GW00758969

The French Revolution

THE BEST ONE-HOUR HISTORY

Robert Freeman

The Best One-Hour History™

Kendall Lane Publishers, Palo Alto, CA

Copyright © 2013, Robert Freeman

All rights reserved.

ISBN-13: 978-0-9892502-1-4

Contents

1 Introduction

In the summer of 1789, the people of France began a Revolution against their government. It started innocently in an effort to balance the nation's budget. But before long, things got radical. The revolutionaries put an end to feudalism. They brought the national church under the control of the state, ousted the king, killed him, and installed a republic. Then things got *really* radical.

The revolutionaries began a "Reign of Terror," killing tens of thousands of their countrymen. Eventually, the Terror consumed its own leaders. The Revolution limped along for another five years until it was ended by a *coup d'etat* in 1799. Napoleon Bonaparte seized power, made himself Emperor, conquered most of Europe, (sometimes under the color of Revolutionary ideals), but was defeated in 1815 as a result of his own overreach.

But as dramatic as the political and military dimensions of the Revolution were, it was much more. It overthrew most of the economic, social and cultural systems of France. At its heart it was a civil war of opposing classes, based on the most militant ideas that had been forming in Europe for the prior century. It espoused the rights of all men, the rule of law, the imperative of uniform justice, the importance of equal opportunity, and the absolute indispensability of individual liberty. It put into practice all of these grand ideas of the European Enlightenment, sometimes artfully, often badly. In doing so, it rocked the foundations of the Western world.

This volume begins with an overview of the Revolution, from its beginning in 1789 to Napoleon's defeat in 1815. It explores the causes of the Revolution, from shallow, proximate causes to deeper, philosophical ones. It details the progression of the Revolution through six distinct governments and discusses some of the enduring themes. Finally, it examines some of the most significant consequences of the Revolution. Those would be profound.

Absolute monarchy would eventually disappear. Feudalism was banished, at least in western Europe. Laws became more uniform while the rule of law became the norm. People gained rights. Nationalism became one of the most potent forces on the planet. And the modern, administrative state was born.

Not all of these things happened immediately and, in fact, most of them were stamped out in the aftermath of Napoleon's defeat. The reactionary victors of the Napoleonic Wars tried to return Europe to the world that existed before the Revolution had begun. But it was too late. The genie was out of the bottle.

The changes wrought by the Revolution, mentioned here and discussed in greater depth below, did happen eventually—inevitably—as a result of the Revolution. In fact, so great was their collective impact on the political, legal, military, social, cultural, and economic systems of the Western world, the French Revolution must be counted as one of the most significant events of the last thousand years.

2 Overview

The French Revolution was a violent convulsion that aligned the formal social, legal, economic and administrative institutions of France with the realities of its present day. France of 1789 was in some ways still in the Middle Ages. It was ruled by a very small portion of the population—the monarchy, aristocracy, and clergy—much as it had been for the prior 1,000 years. The members of these bodies enjoyed enormous social standing and possessed great wealth (mostly inherited), but paid virtually nothing in taxes. They lived in a feudal relation with the rest of French society, living decadently by extracting the surplus wealth that was produced by everyone else.

But in 1788, the government went bankrupt. It had exhausted its funds in decades of wars, extravagant living, and avoidance of taxes by those with the means to pay. The king's ministers tried to get the aristocrats to help pay for the operation of the government, but they refused. This impasse between the aristocracy and the monarchy forced the government to call into session the Estates General in order to reconceive the nation's unwritten constitution. The Estates General purportedly represented all of the people of France but had not met for 173 years, since 1614. The world had changed enormously in that time. So, once the meeting convened, in May 1789, things exploded.

Immediately, a new class of actors that had barely existed in 1614—the *bourgeoisie*—seized control of the meeting. They called themselves the National Assembly and claimed to speak for the nation. They intimidated the king into endorsing that position. Once in power, the National Assembly began overturning the old order. It abolished the feudal system, placed the church under the control of the state, reorganized the nation's medieval administrative systems, and enacted laws to promote equality as a social ideal. These actions and, more importantly, the ideas behind them, constituted a radical assault on the very nature of French society. They were threatening to the other monarchies of Europe as well.

By 1792, the government was under attack from within and without. It was at war with the other nations of Europe. More ominous, the king, Louis XVI, was discovered conspiring with other monarchs to overturn the Revolution. So, the revolutionaries, now acting as the National Convention, killed the king but then faced a counter-revolutionary backlash from those who had supported him. In response, the

Convention instituted a Reign of Terror where state power was exercised by a newly created Committee of Public Safety. The Committee was led by Maximilien Robespierre of the left-leaning Jacobin party. Political opponents were murdered en masse, speculators were hanged, revolts were violently suppressed, all while the government was carrying out its wars abroad.

Eventually the drama and the trauma became too great. The society was exhausted. Robespierre was killed in 1794 by revolutionaries even more radical than himself and the government lapsed into years of muddling through. The Convention expired with the creation of a newly-formed Directory. The economy was a wreck, civil strife was endemic, wars continued to rage, and a series of *coups d'etat*, both by and against the government led, in 1799, to a final *coup d'etat* and the imposition of a military dictatorship under the rule of Napoleon Bonaparte.

Bonaparte would take the Revolution on the road, invading and conquering most of the other nations of Europe. But after a disastrous invasion of Russia in 1812, he was defeated at the battle of Leipzig in 1813, and was forced to abdicate. He was banished to the island of Elba in the Mediterranean but escaped and returned for 100 days. He was finally defeated at the battle of Waterloo in 1815. At the Congress of Vienna, the victors reinstated the Bourbon monarchy under Louis XVIII and tried to impose reactionary regimes across Europe in order to roll back the clock to where it had been before 1789.

But the bourgeois Revolution, by then 26 years on, could not be undone. It left a legacy of republicanism, secularism, nationalism, and capitalism. By these standards, the French Revolution can arguably be considered the birthplace of the modern world.

3 Causes

Most truly momentous historical events have causes that are deep, broad, powerful, complex, and enduring. This is certainly true in the case of the French Revolution. Among the immediate causes of the Revolution were the bankruptcy of the government and the unwillingness of the aristocracy to bear a greater share in its costs. More fundamental causes were changes in demographics over the prior century, the emergence of a new class of actors in society, the *bourgeoisie*, and a new philosophical milieu that we call the Enlightenment. Whether long-lived or short, shallow or deep, this cocktail of causes came to a head in 1789 with the convening of the Estates General.

Proximate Causes

By 1789, all of Europe seemed ripe for some kind of change. Over the prior century, improvements in agricultural techniques and changes in feudal relations had released millions of peasants from the land. These peasants became migrant workers—

"teeming masses"—who found their way into the cities in search of work or welfare. Income and wealth had become enormously unequal, with a small minority of the population living in opulence and the rest in squalor. The prevailing cultural climate was critical of the abuses of monarchy and nobility and fed the resentment of the masses.

At the same time, Europe had just witnessed the revolution in America where colonists had won their own country after having been denied fair representation in the English Parliament. Imagine, then, the anger of the French population, in realizing how much worse off they must be, for they didn't even *have* a Parliament, or anybody to represent their interests in the government. Such sentiment was not confined to France, either. In the year before the start of the French Revolution, smaller revolts against abusive power had occurred in neighboring Holland and Belgium. Both of these revolts emboldened the French in starting their own.

Rigid Ancien Regime

The established order in France—the *ancien regime*—had endured since medieval times. It consisted of the monarchy and three "Estates." The First Estate, the clergy, was embodied in the Catholic Church and traced its lineage back to the days of Charlemagne. The church owned 10% of all the land in France and received huge incomes from the compulsory tithes of its parishioners. The clergy numbered about 200,000 people, or less than one percent of the population. The Second Estate, the nobility, comprised about 300,000 people, a little more than one percent of the population. It owned most of the land and received substantial income from its rent and from payment by peasants of fees that could be traced to feudal times. Finally, the Third Estate was composed of all others, primarily the peasantry. The Third Estate made up some 97% of the population.

There were two significant problems with this structure. The first was that it provided no account of the recently emerged *bourgeoisie*, the new class of citizens associated with the rise of capitalism: shopkeepers; merchants; factory owners; lawyers; bureaucrats; doctors; artisans; and such. This class of citizens had become increasingly important in French society since the emergence of towns in the Middle Ages. But they had no recognition for their contribution to the country and no avenues by which to participate in the running of the society. They wanted higher social status and representation in government.

The second, larger, problem was that neither the clergy nor the nobility paid anything like its share of taxes—nor did they want to. Earlier Bourbon kings, beginning with Louis XIII, had exempted the nobility from taxes in order to buy their complicity in their autocratic rule. So, almost all of the costs of operating the government were borne by the peasantry who not only paid taxes to the king, but tithes to the church, and land rent and feudal fees to the nobility. Even in the face of the fiscal crisis facing the monarchy, both the nobility and the clergy were adamant that they would not pay any increased taxes. It was this refusal—and the bankruptcy of the government that it occasioned—that forced Louis XVI to call the meeting of the Estates General.

Economic Problems

Compounding the financial problems, economic conditions in France had become increasingly hard for most of the people. The population had expanded throughout the century but there was no additional land to feed it. Then, several bad harvests in the late 1780s left many peasants without food. Bread riots erupted throughout the country. To make matters worse, the nobility, which had been hurt by a century-long European-wide price inflation, had begun to take back land that had been held for centuries "in common" by all members of a village. The peasantry relied on such commons for a significant part of their sustenance. Enclosures, therefore, increased the peasants' resentment of the *ancien regime.*

Also, the *bourgeoisie* had become extremely dissatisfied with the management of the economy. The monarchy's loss of the Seven Years War to England in 1763 and the consequent loss of colonies in North America and Asia meant merchants had fewer opportunities to sell products abroad. Worse,

France was flooded with manufactured products from England, which was more advanced than France in its adoption of emerging industrial technology. These forces threatened the *bourgeoisie's* prosperity and its tenuous standing in the all-important social order. In other words, all classes of French people, from the richest to the poorest and all those in between, were unhappy with current economic conditions. The entire country was ripe for change.

Philosophical Foundations

The philosophical milieu known as The Enlightenment exerted a great influence on intellectuals and the French middle class. They became convinced that the existing order was hopelessly flawed and irretrievably corrupt. They believed that if the ideas of Locke, Montesquieu, Rousseau, Voltaire and others were put into practice (as they seemed to have been in the recently-formed United States), a more orderly and just society could be built.

Specifically, this literate class believed that men had been created equal by God and that distinctions based on birth (the basis of the nobility) were unnatural and unjust. They believed that men had natural rights and that the purpose of government was to protect those rights. Many believed that the Catholic Church was a corrupt institution, peddling superstition, fear, and guilt, and that it should be abolished or severely constrained. They believed that laws should be applied equally to all men, regardless of wealth or social standing. And they almost universally believed that reason could guide the construction and operation of government. These beliefs were at complete odds with the existing order. They formed the intellectual justification for the overthrow of the French government.

Bankrupt Monarchy

The event that actually triggered the start of the Revolution was the bankruptcy of the monarchy. For the prior 150 years, French kings had carried out an orgy of spending on dynastic wars in Europe, wars for territorial expansion, colonial competition with England, and wildly extravagant living. The monarchy had exhausted not only its money but its credit as well. Finance ministers had tried to arrange loans in 1787 to keep the foundering government afloat, but could not manage to secure the funds. In the summer of 1788, the government could not make the interest payments on past loans and went bankrupt. It had no choice but to find new sources of income.

To do so, it convened the Estates General, an historic assembly that was supposed to represent the interests of all of the French people. There, it hoped to convince the Three Estates to approve additional tax revenues to the king. But by 1789, the Estates General had not met for 175 years, since 1614. Much had changed since that time, not the least of which was the power of the emergent middle class—the *bourgeoisie*—and the hostility of the peasantry to the monarchy and aristocracy. Once convened, the Estates General proved impossible for the king to control. The representatives of the Third Estate, whom Louis had assumed he could intimidate, refused to be cowed. Instead, they insisted that they spoke for the whole of the French people—the nation. It was this defiant insistence that sparked the beginning of the Revolution.

4 Six Different Governments

That the Revolution was chaotic is an understatement. From its beginning in 1789 to its end in 1799, six different governments operated in France. They were as follows:

Government	Dates	Political Nature
Monarchy	pre-1789	Monarchy
National Assembly	1789-1791	Proto-Constitutional Monarchy
Legislative Assembly	1791-1792	Constitutional Monarchy
National Convention	1792-1795	Republic/Dictatorship by Terror
Directory	1795-1799	Republic/Dictatorship by Committee
Consulate-Empire	1799-1815	Empire

These different governments spanned the political spectrum from conservative to liberal to radical and back again. This "arc of ideology"—traversed back and forth in only 10 years—is one of the most distinguishing characteristics of the Revolution.

Monarchy (pre-1789)

Louis XVI was the monarch who ruled France at the beginning of the French Revolution. He had assumed the throne in 1754 on the eve of the Seven Years War with England and Prussia. Louis was a somewhat dim-witted ruler, but one who believed in the divine right of kings, as did most European monarchs of that time. He spent more than he had but when he could not convince either the nobility or the clergy to increase their payment of taxes to support his lavish lifestyle, and when creditors would no longer loan money to make up the difference, he had no choice but to call the Estates General into session. It would prove a fateful decision.

National Assembly (1789 – 1791)

When the Estates General convened on May 1, 1789, members of the Third Estate refused to accept Louis' rules for how their votes would be counted. Though peasants and the *bourgeoisie* made up some 97% of the population of France, Louis proposed that each Estate should have one vote, i.e., that the clergy and nobility, with less 3% of the population between them, should have 67% of the votes. Instead, the representatives of the Third Estate announced that they spoke not simply for the peasants, workers, and *bourgeoisie*, but for *all* of the people of France.

On June 17th, they declared themselves the National Assembly. Louis refused to accept this self-appointed status and on June 20th had them evicted. They moved to a local tennis court where they took the famous "Tennis Court Oath," declaring they would not disband until France had a constitution and a new form of government. Within a week, Louis capitulated and on June 27th, recognized the National Assembly as the representative of the French people. Louis would continue to sit on the throne until he was killed in 1793, but it was the beginning of the end of monarchical rule.

Storming of the Bastille. In early July, 1789, military forces surrounded Paris. The people of Paris believed these forces had been called by Louis to disband the National Assembly. In fact, they had. Louis had given in to the demands of the Third Estate, hoping to buy time until the ring-leaders could be arrested. Determined to stop such an event, a group of some 900-odd radicals marched to the Bastille, an ancient prison in the heart of the city. Believing it contained ammunition, they forced their way inside, killed the guards, and freed the seven prisoners. There was no ammunition and the event itself had no military significance at all. But it caught the imagination of the French people. The King had lost control of his capital to an inflamed and defiant citizenry. Still today, Bastille Day, July 14, 1789, is considered the day of Independence in France, equivalent to July 4th, 1776 in the United States.

Declaration of the Rights of Man and Citizen. One of the first acts of the National Assembly was to publish the *Declaration of the Rights of Man and Citizen* declaring the philosophical basis for the Revolution. The document was written by the Marquis de Lafayette who had been an aide to George Washington during the American Revolutionary War. He was assisted by Thomas Jefferson. The ideas expressed in the *Declaration* are straight out of the Enlightenment. They include such "simple and incontestable principles" as these: people have natural rights; government derives its legitimacy from the consent of the governed; law is the expression of the "general will" of the people; people are innocent until proven guilty; people are entitled to religious freedom; no taxation without representation; and freedom of the press. Much of the *Declaration's* content was adopted by the United Nations in its founding charter of 1946.

Most of the positive achievements of the Revolution were begun by the National Assembly. For example, it extended the right to vote to all property-owning males. It re-organized the highly fragmented administrative system that had governed France since the Middle Ages and which perpetuated both local particularism and the privileges of the nobility and clergy. In its place, it created a structure of nested administrative bodies that is similar to that still used today. Instead of government service based on privilege where the rich paid to obtain an office, a much more democratically-oriented system was created where titles were assigned according to election and merit. And, to end the injustice of France's enduring feudal legacy, it outlawed all feudal fees and customs, subject to compensation of the dispossessed.

To address the country's financial problems (and to diminish the role of the church in the state), the National Assembly confiscated the lands of the Catholic Church and offered them for sale to the country's people. It issued a paper currency based on the value of these lands. So many of these "assignats" were issued, they soon became worthless. Nevertheless, these accomplishments, because of their import, their scope, and the fact that they were achieved through a peaceful and democratic process while the country was at peace, represented the legislative high point of the Revolution.

The Flight to Varennes. Louis XVI had nothing but disdain for the revolutionaries. He had treated them shabbily when they first met as the Estates General and even when he had been held as virtual prisoner from October 1789 at the Tuilleires palace in Paris. On the night of June 20, 1791, Louis and his wife, Marie Antoinette, tried to escape the country. They got as far as the town of Varennes near the border with Luxembourg before they were recognized by a postal worker and stopped. They were returned to Paris and placed under house arrest.

The attempted escape created deep divisions within the National Assembly. It forced royalists, constitutional monarchists, and republicans to draw lines that all had assumed had been unnecessary when Louis had pretended to be cooperating. They accelerated their work on a new constitution, which would install the new legislature and make official the status of the country as a constitutional monarchy. The hastily written Constitution of 1791 defined the formal organization of that constitutional monarchy but limited the power of the king to an almost titular role. The new constitution was rushed into effect in October 1791.

Legislative Assembly (1791-1792)

Under the new constitution, legislative powers rested in the newly created Legislative Assembly, which began as soon as elections were completed and the constitution was approved. A "self-denying decree" prevented current members from serving in the new government. This deprived the new government of experienced members, a situation made still worse in that 95% of the new members were from the Third Estate, a group of people with literally no experience in governing. The Legislative Assembly's tenure was to prove brief and traumatic.

First, it was designed to be the legislative arm of a constitutional monarchy. But it came into being in the wake of the King's attempted escape. As such, it was riven with division. On one side were those loyal to the king and a constitutional monarchy. On the other side were those who wanted to overthrow the king and establish a fully independent republic. On still a third side were the royalists who had never wanted a constitution or even a parliament and who plotted incessantly for a return to monarchical rule. The intense mutual hatred between these factions made it virtually impossible for them to work together.

Second, and perhaps more importantly, the Constitution of 1791 was fundamentally flawed. Though it nominally divided government duties between two branches—executive and legislative—in fact, the balance was seriously skewed in favor of the legislature. It had the power to tax, declare war, operate systems of justice, the military, and more. Against this vast assemblage of power, the role of the king was largely symbolic, though he did retain the right of veto. And, since the king had been held virtual prisoner since the beginning of the Legislative Assembly, his perceived importance in the operation of the government was reduced further still. While the Legislative Assembly was faced with these internal problems, it confronted external problems as well.

Revolutionary Wars with Europe. The other countries of Europe did not take well to France's Revolution. They were, after all, monarchies and worried about Revolutionary zeal infecting their own people. In August of 1791, the king of Prussia and the Emperor of Austria issued the *Declaration of Pillnitz,* stating that if Louis was not restored to the throne, they would invade France. They added that if he was harmed they would burn Paris to the ground. This Declaration enraged the citizens of France who saw it as the result of scheming by Louis to try to undo the Revolution.

On April 20, 1792, the Legislative Assembly declared war on Austria (and later on Prussia and Britain as well). Ironically, the war was supported by the center and right-leaning parties but for different reasons. The center party, the Girondin, wanted to export the Revolution to other countries of Europe. The royalists, representing the right, wanted a war so as to bring into being a military government that could return the king to power. The left-leaning party, the Jacobins, led by Maximilian Robespierre, was leery of war. It was wise to the motivation of the royalists, knowing that an army, especially one led by aristocratic officers, could easily be turned on the revolutionary government itself.

Within the year, most of the major powers of Europe were at war with France, a state of affairs that continued more or less without interruption until Napoleon Bonaparte's final defeat in 1815. By these French Wars of Revolution, the leaders of the Revolution plunged the country into a foreign policy crisis at exactly the moment domestic policy was coming undone. The wars drained the already depleted French treasury and increased the sense of siege experienced by the governing revolutionaries.

They would prove the precursors to a Reign of Terror that would consume and ultimately destroy the Revolution.

Following the start of war, the political mood of the Legislative Assembly became more radical. Its temper was inflamed by the "Paris Mob," a group of citizen activists loosely under the direction of the representatives of the local government of Paris. It was among the most radical of all the groups operating during the Revolution. The Legislative Assembly abolished the last remnants of feudal obligations, together with the requirement that nobles be compensated. It consummated the sale of church lands and declared that those nobles who had fled the country would have their property confiscated if they did not return. It approved divorce by mutual consent, a major blow to the longstanding tradition and authority of the Catholic Church.

In July 1792, papers were discovered in Louis' possession that unquestionably tied him to attempts to destroy the Revolution and to reinstall himself in the position of King. This discovery only reinforced the suspicion of the anti-royalists that the King had never sincerely accepted the fact of a constitutional partnership with the Legislature. It gave rise to riots in the capital and forced upon the Legislative Assembly the need to deal with the King's perfidy. However, according to the existing constitution, the Legislative Assembly did not have the authority to implement a Republic. So, they called for the formation of a National Convention to try the King for treason, to decide an appropriate punishment, and to design a new constitution that would launch a full-fledged republic.

National Convention (1792-1795)

The National Convention was seated in September, 1792. Its first major act was to declare the end of the monarchy and the establishment of the French Republic. Its second major act was to put Louis XVI on trial for treason and to sentence him to death. He was killed in January, 1793. This second act divided the Convention along the lines of radicals, who wanted Louis killed, and moderates who were willing to have him simply imprisoned or banished. The more radical elements were known as Jacobins while the more moderate (though still liberal) elements were known as Girondins. Royalists (conservatives) had ceased to play an effective role in the government after the death of the king, with many of them emigrating to other European countries.

When French forces were defeated in early battles against Austria and Prussia, the Jacobins used the occasion to blame the Girondins. It was, after all, the Girondins who had wanted the war in the first place and many of the army's leaders were members of the Girondins. Some generals, members of the nobility, were suspected of leaking troop movements to the enemy in order to precipitate defeat and collapse of the French regime. On this basis, the Jacobins managed to drive the Girondins from the Convention and seize almost uncontested control of the French government. From there, the Revolution took a violent turn. The most energetic elements, spurred on by the Paris Mob, pushed an increasingly radical agenda of social leveling and eradication of all of the artifacts of the old feudal regime.

Civil War as a Prelude to Terror. Despite the Revolution's enticing claims to free all men from tyranny, many Frenchmen preferred the stability of the old order to the chaos of the new. Perhaps even more important, most Frenchmen were still Catholic and resented the Revolution's treatment of the Catholic Church: the forced sale of Church lands; making priests swear loyalty to the government, etc. Many such people rose up against the Republic, especially in western France. There, the people of Vendee, Anjou, Brittany and other provinces refused the call for a military draft and, instead, raised armies and marched against the government. The government's response was swift and brutal.

Tens of thousands of "counter-revolutionary" Frenchmen were killed. The city of Lyon, a hotbed of resistance, was shelled and destroyed. In Nantes, two thousand rebels were drowned when the barges on which they were imprisoned were intentionally sunk. The rebellion struck fear into the hearts of the radicals who were at the head of the government. They worried their Revolution was at risk not only from without, at the hands of other nations, but, now, from within, at the hands of French counter-revolutionaries. They hardened their commitment to their program of reform and implemented the bloodiest, most notorious episode of the entire Revolution.

The Reign of Terror. In the summer of 1793, the Jacobin-dominated National Convention instituted a campaign of state-sponsored terror known as the Reign of Terror. Its intent was both to purge France of counter-revolutionaries and intimidate prospective resisters. The Committee of Public Safety was formed by the Convention to carry out executions of all suspected royalists as well as anyone who lacked proper "virtue," i.e., did not obey the arbitrary dictates of the Committee. More than 500,000 such "suspects" were put in jail. It was full scale war by the government against anyone who challenged its radical policies or its absolute authority.

The guillotine became the most famous symbol of the Terror. Under its blade, more than 2,000 people were beheaded in Paris alone. The death toll throughout the country exceeded 20,000 as ever more violence was employed to try to suppress opposition. The Committee's leader, Maximilien Robespierre, was effectively dictator of France from late 1793 until July 1794 when he lost control of the Terror and became one of its victims. The Terror did more than anything else to turn reasonable people of Europe against the Revolution. Its ruthless, bloody tactics would be copied by totalitarian dictatorships in the twentieth century including those of Stalin in Russia, Mao in China and Pol Pot in Cambodia.

The Convention accomplished more than simply murder and mayhem, though that is what it is principally known for. It outlawed imprisonment for debt. It ended primogeniture, the practice of the oldest son inheriting all of his father's estate. And it introduced the metric system—a legacy of the Enlightenment's emphasis on reason as a guide to building an orderly and just society. Still, the social fabric of the country was irreparably torn. The conservative countryside abhorred the radicalism of Paris. Catholics hated the secularist government and the disenfranchisement of the Church. Republicans constantly suspected royalists of trying to undermine the revolution and install a new king to power.

The death of Robespierre marked not just the end of the Terror but the return to a more moderate form of government. The Girondins were reinstated, though tensions between them and the Jacobins remained high. The Committee of Public Safety was disbanded, many Jacobin clubs were closed, and price controls on basic commodities such as bread were ended. The Convention wrote still one more constitution, the Constitution of 1795 and then disbanded itself and ushered in the next government, the Directory.

The Directory (1795-1799)

Following the bloody and hysterical tenure of the Convention, the Directory was somewhat anti-climactic. After six years of violence, tumult, and rancor, people wanted stability, calm, and orderliness. And, the Directory's challenges were enormous: stabilize the economy; restore a working monetary system (the previous one had broken down); defend the country from attacks by other European powers; and implement new electoral and administrative reforms. Amazingly, they had to try to do all of this while maintaining the true spirit and liberalizing fervor of the Revolution. These tasks proved too much.

The Directory's structure was similar to that of a republic: an Executive consisting of five members; and a two-house legislature, The Council of Ancients, and the Council of Five Hundred. In practice, however, The Directory soon became a dictatorship by committee, not unlike the Convention that preceded it, though without the violence. It first refused to seat Councilors who were too conservative—that is, too inclined to restore the monarchy. Then, it refused to seat those who were too radical—those who wanted universal suffrage and an end to the property rights requirement for voting. It was trying to steer a middle course, to preserve the Republican gains of the Revolution, but to return some of the institutions that had implicitly ordered society for hundreds of years.

In the elections of March 1797, the aristocrats mounted a major organizing and propaganda campaign emphasizing the need for a return to order. It was hugely successful, with two thirds of the elected deputies supporting the royalist cause. But the elections were overturned by an internal *coup* in September, known as *Fructidor*. Royalist supporters were denied seating in the legislative chambers, but neo-Jacobins were denied seating as well. The Directory had betrayed its claims to liberal inclusion and was operating as an unconstitutional dictatorship. It had lost the respect and support of virtually the whole of French society, a fact that contributed to its being overthrown in the final *coup* of the Revolution.

Napoleon's coup d'etat of Brumaire. In the end, the Directory's ineffectiveness proved its undoing. By early 1799, military gains in Italy and Germany were reversed and foreign enemies stood poised to invade France. In October 1799, Napoleon Bonaparte returned from wars in Egypt. In November 1799 (*Brumaire* according to the Revolutionary calendar), he conspired with two members of the Directory to overthrow the government and install a military dictatorship called the Consulate. Their pretext for seizing power was a Jacobin plot against the government. When some Councilors challenged Napoleon's story, the *coup* was almost thwarted. However, Napoleon's brother, Lucien, convinced the army to seize the meeting hall at St. Cloud where the Council of Five Hundred was meeting. The *coup* then succeeded. France was now ruled by a military dictatorship. The Revolution was dead.

The Directory had been the last experiment in republican rule. Its expiration marked the end of the French Revolution. It had accomplished some good: it prevented France from being taken over by other European countries; and it began the world's first practice of public primary education. But it had also faltered in some fundamental ways. It had failed to make peace with the other countries of Europe. It allowed the reconsolidation of power into the hands of the few. And it returned France to the more stratified social order that had been one of the impetuses of the Revolution in the first place. In these ways, the Directory left France somewhat worse off than it had been before its tenure had begun.

Consulate and the Age of Napoleon (1799-1815)

The Napoleonic era is not considered a formal part of the French Revolution, for it returned France to the rule of a single, autocratic, hereditary ruler of the same ilk that the Revolution had overthrown in 1792. But it is included here to indicate how it was that the larger Revolutionary era ended.

Napoleon Bonaparte had been a successful general fighting for the French Republic throughout the Revolution. He won a highly visible fight with the British at the port city of Toulon in 1794 and defended the National Convention against an angry mob in 1795. He was extraordinarily successful in military campaigns in Italy against the armies of Austria and Prussia and, as a result, became a national hero.

The *coup* of *Brumaire* dissolved the Directory, and in its place put a three-man council (the Consulate), which was little more than a front for a military dictatorship. Within a short time, Napoleon overthrew his two co-conspirators in the *coup* and in 1802, gave himself the title, "First Consul for Life." In 1804, he dispensed with all fictions of democratic rule and named himself Emperor with the right to pass on the title to a relative. Napoleon would reign (with a short, nine month interruption in 1814) until 1815 when he was defeated at the Battle of Waterloo.

Napoleon was, above all else, a military man and that proved his downfall. Under the guise of exporting the revolutionary ideas of France, he invaded and conquered most of the other nations of Europe. In a daring series of campaigns, he occupied Italy, Spain, Germany, Austria, and invaded Russia, putting most of them under the control of French rulers, many of them his relatives. These countries, funded by Britain (who also fought against Napoleon) formed a number of "coalitions" to fight Napoleon but most failed. In 1812, Napoleon invaded Russia with an army of 600,000 men. The vast expanse, overextended supply lines, vigorous nationalistic response, and bleak winter contributed to Napoleon's greatest defeat. By the time he left Russia, in December 1812, he had only 25,000 men left in his army. Tchaikovsky's memorable *1812 Overture*, with its bugle charges and booming cannons, was composed to commemorate the Russian victory.

The collective powers of Europe, seeing Napoleon's vulnerability after Russia, allied themselves to defeat him at the Battle of Leipzig in 1813. They offered him surrender terms, first on the basis of France's 1799 borders, and then within France's 1792 borders, but he refused. He was exiled to the small Mediterranean island of Elba. He escaped Elba in February, 1815, returned to France, raised another army, and began attacking Europe again. One hundred days later, Napoleon was finally defeated by British and Prussian forces at the Battle of Waterloo in Belgium in June 1815. He was exiled to the island of St. Helena in the south Atlantic where he died in 1821.

During the fifteen-odd years of Napoleon's rule, he instituted major changes in French society, many of which had enduring influence on other European countries. Among other things, he dramatically redesigned the French legal code, making it one of the most egalitarian in all the world; streamlined the nation's administrative system; implemented a new university system; created the Bank of France; crafted a reconciliation with the Pope; sold the Louisiana Territory to America (Jefferson's Louisiana

Purchase); and made the tax code fairer to all classes of citizens. Importantly, Napoleon began a policy that government and military officials would be promoted not on the basis of their hereditary title, but rather on the basis of merit, a policy he had used and proven in his military days.

The sum of these policies represented revolutionary change in how governments operated, ending the policies of privilege-based, aristocratic-centered government that had prevailed in most of Europe since the Middle Ages.

5 Iconic Themes

Iconic events produce iconic themes. The Renaissance is synonymous with artistic genius; World War I with trench warfare. The French Revolution produced its own iconic themes, many of which echo in the popular lexicon still today: Liberty, Equality, Fraternity; bourgeois culture; mob rule; church and state. It is worth noting the role these ideas played in the unfolding of the Revolution.

Liberty, Equality, Fraternity

In 1790, Robespierre proposed including the words, "Liberty, Equality, Fraternity," on the uniforms of French soldiers. Though the proposal was turned down at the time, the phrase ultimately became the quintessential expression of the Revolution. The ideas of liberty and equality came directly from the Enlightenment. Liberty was the way that reason got put into practice. Equality was the antithesis of the stratified social order that it had been one of the Revolution's aims to destroy. Together, these fired the imagination, not only of Frenchmen, but of people throughout Europe.

Fraternity was more subtle. Fraternity means "brotherhood" and symbolized the idea that all men live together in community. In a sense, Fraternity moderates the excesses of Liberty, for, left without limit, Liberty will almost certainly destroy Equality. (The ancient Greeks restricted liberty for precisely this reason.) But by being combined with Fraternity, Liberty and Equality produce a social ideal where men can live as members of a larger human family, equal and free as men, but concerned with the well-being of each other. During the Empire, the phrase was suppressed but it returned in the Constitution of 1848 and was officially declared the essential spirit of the French people in the Constitution of 1958.

A Bourgeois Revolution

The word "Revolution" evokes images of peasants with pitchforks storming castles. But as familiar as that image may be, the French Revolution was something different. It was largely the making of the recently emerged French middle class, the *bourgeoisie*. And as much as the king was the symbol of its wrath, it was equally aimed against the abuses of the nobility. The Revolution was the epochal struggle of the newly ascendant capitalist order against the aged and dying feudal order.

The "*bourgeois*-centric" character of the revolution is reflected in its philosophical foundation, the

Declaration of the Rights of Man and Citizen. There, the "imprescriptible rights of man" are defined as, "...liberty, property, security, and resistance to oppression." (Compare this with the U.S. Declaration's listing of critical rights as, "life, liberty and the pursuit of happiness.") In the French Declaration's final article it states, "Since property is an inviolable and sacred right, no one shall be deprived thereof..." This concern for property was also reflected in the character and the actions of the successive governments and people who carried out the Revolution.

All of the governments, from the National Assembly to the Directory, were dominated by the *bourgeoisie.* The right to sit in those governments was based on one's ownership of property, and the right to vote—the franchise—was also accorded only to owners of property. Even the Paris Mob, so influential in so many decisions affecting the Revolution's outcome, was dominated by radical members of the middle class. In its constant focus on property rights, including to the exclusion of liberty, the French Revolution marked the signal turning point in the millennial changing of economic systems, from the one that had dominated for the past thousand years—feudalism—to the one which would define the future of the Western world—capitalism.

Influence of the Paris Mob

The most radical—and perhaps influential—of all the organizations during the French Revolution was the Paris Mob. It was called by various names—the Paris Commune, the Commune—but it was always present to menace lawmakers and influence outcomes during the Revolution. For example, the agitators who formed the Commune were the same who organized the storming of the Bastille. It was the Commune which forced the Legislative Assembly to call the National Convention for the purpose of trying (and eventually executing) Louis XVI. It was the Mob that pressured the Convention to repudiate the monarchy and declare France a republic.

Time and again, when government leaders attempted a moderate course for national policy, a course more representative of the thoughts of people outside of Paris, they were intimidated from doing so by the radical members of the Mob. It has been said that 3,000 people (a rough estimate of the number of active Paris radicals) learned how to hold hostage 30,000,000 (the population of France). It is an astounding fact that such a small number of unelected troublemakers could control the destiny of so many, but the power of focused violence, especially in the context of chaos, should not be underestimated. The Mob's techniques would later be emulated by Vladimir Lenin during the early days of the Russian Revolution in 1917.

Conflicts Over the Catholic Church

Probably no other issue caused so much conflict within France during the Revolution as did the treatment of the Catholic Church. In 1790, to help pay the bills of the government, the National Assembly confiscated the lands of the Church and offered them for sale. At the same time, it ordered that all Roman Catholic clergy become employees of the state and swear an oath of allegiance to the French Republic. To the Catholic clergy, this was heresy. Their loyalty was to the Pope whom they considered God's representative on earth. To the masses of French peasants who were overwhelmingly Catholic, the clergy reporting to the government was incomprehensible.

Revolts broke out in protest, primarily in western France. These were ruthlessly suppressed by the government. Later, during the Reign of Terror, the effort to de-Christianize France went even further, with the Committee of Public Safety proposing a "Cult of the Supreme Being" as the French national church. This idea died with Robespierre in 1794 but resentment and hostility festered until 1801 when Napoleon reached an official *Concordat* with the Vatican which acknowledged Catholicism as the religion of the majority of the French people. It was precisely the recognition of such deep tensions between church and state—tensions that in some cases went back more than 1000 years—that caused the American founders to try to separate the two in the Bill of Rights to the U.S. Constitution.

The Limitations of "Reason"

It is one of the enduring enigmas of the French Revolution that for so much of what it intended to do, it ended up doing exactly the opposite. It wanted to be a nation of reason but ended up being a nation of terror. It wanted to establish governance by the rule of law. Instead, it created chaos. It began with the desire to increase liberty and ended with vastly more repression than it had ever started with. And it planned to establish a government of people who had natural rights. Instead, it ended up as a dictatorship of one person with no rights for anyone else. In so many of its ideals it failed completely. How could this be? Several answers come to mind.

First, people are not as reasonable as they imagine themselves to be. Without an objective standard to rely on, one man's reason is another man's folly. For example, is it reasonable to execute those whom you truly believe are trying to destroy the Revolution? This is what the Jacobins did during the Reign of Terror. Also, when people (and nations) are attacked, either from within or from without (or both!), they revert to animal instinct and react more in anger and fear than by reflection and reason. Still, though, they cloak their actions in the justification of Reason. All of this occurred during the Revolution.

Equally important, the Revolution promoted liberty over the rule of law, and change over the maintenance of order. In doing so, it created an internal contradiction that almost guaranteed conflict and the emergence of chaos. This was the Englishman Edmund Burke's criticism of the Revolution—that it placed too much power in the hands of individuals and showed not enough concern for the forces that "conserve" order in society. In 1790, in his famous book, *Reflections on the Revolution in France*, Burke predicted that the Revolution would degenerate into violence, for with no stable standard to tether itself to, it would become hijacked by the most radical elements. Burke's predictions proved true and his views became the basis of conservative political philosophy which still operates today.

6   Lasting Consequences

It is the consequences of the French Revolution that signify its status as one of the most important events of the last thousand years. These extend to the political, administrative, and economic realms, and cast their effect on virtually all countries on earth. Though some were reversed in the immediate aftermath of the Revolution, they eventually defined what we consider the hallmarks of the modern world.

The End of French Dominance in Europe

In 1763, as a result of its loss in the Seven Years War, France lost the position of "most powerful country in the world" to England. Then, as a result of the French Revolution, even France's position within continental Europe fell dramatically. Never again would it dominate European affairs as it had done before 1763 and during the Revolution. The Congress of Vienna, which established the terms of settlement following Napoleon's defeat, strengthened all the countries surrounding France. It combined Belgium with Holland in the north, the Rhineland with Prussia in the east, gave parts of Italy to Austria in the southeast, and several of France's former colonies to England, all with the goal of surrounding France in order to prevent future aggression. Additionally, France was occupied by armies of the victorious powers. In military terms, France was rendered impotent.

But the real impact on France's fortunes was economic. The war had decimated the French people and their economy. In 1800, France produced 4% of total world manufacturing output compared with 3.5% for Germany and 4% for England. In other words, they were roughly equal. But by 1900, while France's share had grown to 7% Germany's had risen to 13% and England's had exploded to 19%. In coal production, a tangible measure of industrial might, Germany and France produced roughly the same amount in 1800. But by 1900, Germany was producing six times the amount that France was. By virtually every measure of national strength, France, once the leader of Europe, would soon be surpassed by other countries. Its days as the leader of the Western world were over.

The Final End to Feudalism

From the beginning, one of the goals of the Revolution was to end the feudal system which had existed in France for over a thousand years and which continued to hold millions of people in economic bondage. The most notorious practices of feudalism—indenture to the land, payment of fees for use of common resources, assumption to title by birth, etc.—were formally outlawed by the National Assembly in the famous *Decree Abolishing the Feudalism System* of August 4th, 1790.

By the time the Revolution was over and the reign of Napoleon had ended, France had instituted formal systems of merit for elevation to all important political offices. This was the first time this had ever occurred. More importantly, with the rise of the *bourgeoisie*, the sanctification of private property, and the onset of the Industrial Revolution in the late eighteenth and early nineteenth centuries, the anachronism of feudalism never resurfaced again in Western Europe. It did, however, endure in Eastern Europe before being abolished in the second half of the nineteenth century.

Conservative Reaction and the Emergence of Constitutional Government

The cultural and political upheaval of the Revolution provoked a sharply conservative reaction from the rulers of Europe. They were determined to not allow such incendiary folly to erupt again. At the Congress of Vienna, which began in 1814, they instituted a rigidly monarchist regime throughout continental Europe. Its intent was to suppress any of the liberal or nationalist impulses that had given them such trouble over the prior 25 years. Liberalism was a threat to monarchical government. Nationalism was a threat to empire. The

Concert of Europe oversaw the implementation of the autocratic Congress of Vienna system under the leadership of Prince Metternich of Austria. It operated as a monarchs' club to enforce conservative political regimes for most of the early nineteenth century.

But the liberalizing genie, once let out of the bottle, proved difficult to put back in. Once people got a taste of representation and constitutional government, they did not want to go back to the autocratic monarchical regimes of the past. The Concert of Europe suppressed liberal revolts in Spain and Italy but by 1830, France erupted into another mini-Revolution, overthrowing another Bourbon king, Charles X. By mid-century, the demands for constitutional government by the people of Europe could no longer be stifled. The year 1848 witnessed revolutions in France, Austria, Hungary, Poland, Italy, Germany and Switzerland. Once again, they were put down but by the end of the century, virtually all of the countries of Europe were under some form of constitutional government. Europe had completed a millennial transition from monarchism to constitutionalism. Its accomplishment would serve as an example to all of the rest of the world.

The Rise of Nationalism
Nationalism occurs when people's primary social identification is with the nation, rather than with their religion or class or fief or some other entity. The Revolution saw a dramatic increase in the number

of people who identified themselves as Frenchmen and who were willing to sacrifice (including die) for the benefit of their nation. Europe had never seen such an intense force before. The generals who fought against French armies were astounded at the ferocity of Frenchmen fighting to defend their country. Many times in battle, it was this intensity alone which allowed a smaller, inferior army to defeat a larger, superior force. In the aftermath of the French Revolution, nationalism became one of the most potent political forces on the planet.

By 1850, more than 50 revolutions had taken place throughout Europe, many of them nationalist in character. Nationalism resulted in the creation of the Italian and German states, in 1861 and 1871, respectively. Nationalism was one of the principal causes of World War I. It would become one of the main forces that, in the 1900s, liberated most of the African continent from European colonial domination. It is what inspired China to throw out European colonists in the beginning of the twentieth century. And it was nationalism that inspired the people of Vietnam, in the 1970s, to overthrow occupation and defeat the armies of the greatest military power in the world, the United States.

The Birth of the Modern Administrative State

The political system of organization we know today as the modern administrative state, where power is centralized in a single, national body, was greatly advanced by the French Revolution and the reign of Napoleon. A universal system of justice (the Napoleonic Code) replaced over 360 different local codes that had been in force before 1789. A streamlined and equitable system of taxation was created and enforced throughout the country. Nation-wide public education (replacing church-sponsored education) was begun with common standards for all grades throughout the country. But as much as anything else, it was the revolution in military affairs that accelerated the growth of this centralized administrative state.

One of the first universal drafts—the *levee en masse*—was implemented to help France in its wars with the other nations of Europe. The whole idea of the "war economy," where the government controls wages, prices, outputs, and other economic decisions, dominated France under the Directory and even more so under Napoleon. The idea that war was not just "diplomacy by other means" but, rather, an integral component of state policy and political control received a significant boost during the Revolution. Most of these innovations in state control—economic, legal, educational, military and judicial—remain as characteristics of all national governments today.

The (temporary) End of Enlightenment

The hopes of the Enlightenment for building a society based on reason were dashed by the excesses of the Revolution. In the aftermath of the Revolution, people attacked as naïve the belief of Enlightenment philosophers that men could act rationally in groups or that a perfect society could be built by mimicking nature. Instead, philosophers, beginning with Kant and Goethe in Germany, began to elevate sentiment and passion to the highest position of human faculties. Logic gave way to beauty. Reason became subsumed to imagination. Analysis yielded to passion. Thought was replaced by feeling.

In all the arts—from music to poetry to literature to painting—this new way of knowing the world became a popular avenue for human expression. In music, the passion and power of Beethoven's *Ode to Joy* replaced the order and formalism of Bach, Hayden, and Mozart. In literature, the burning emotions of *Jane Eyre* became favored over the rigid social norms of eighteenth century society. Byron, Coleridge, Keats, Wordsworth and Shelley became exemplars in poetry. Passion, eroticism, sentimentality, empathy, sorrow, and affection—the whole range of emotions—now exalted the human being. This romance with feeling was precisely a reaction and protest against the elevated and strained intellectualism of the Enlightenment. What began in the passion and fury of the French Revolution became the dominant philosophical and artistic mood of Europe for much of the first half of the next century.

7 Final Word

It is difficult to overstate the impact the French Revolution had on Western Civilization, indeed on all the world's civilizations. Absolute monarchy suffered a serious—and eventually fatal—blow. Within two generations, it would be replaced throughout much of Europe by constitutionalism, either in the form of constitutional monarchies, or republics. Similarly, the thousand-plus year reign of feudalism ended, though it continued in Eastern Europe for another eighty years. It was replaced by capitalism as the dominant organizing economic system of western societies.

The fiefdom structure of the Middle Ages, with its political atomization and aristocratic particularism, gave way to the modern administrative state with an emphasis on rational state management and meritocracy. In a parallel transformation, nationalism replaced parochialism as the lens through which Europeans viewed their political world. The role of the Catholic Church as one of the triad of institutions that had governed Europe for over a thousand years was dramatically reduced, with secularism replacing clericalism as the dominant ideology. Civil rights were enshrined into law. And the modern heroic leader (Napoleon) emerged from this brief period and its amazing events.

Republicanism. Capitalism. Nationalism. Secularism. Civil Rights. These are the institutional hallmarks of what we call the "modern world." Though the forces of change that produced these institutions had been in gestation for several centuries, and though some of them had already emerged in partial form in different places, it was during the trauma and tumult of the French Revolution that they were finally birthed, all together, in full form, in one place, at the same time. It is for this reason that historians point to the French Revolution as the beginning of the modern world.

8 Timeline

1754-1789 **Monarchy** of Louis XVI

1789   May. Estates General convenes at Versailles

June. Third Estate declares it represents the "nation" as a "National Assembly"

June. Louis evicts Third Estate; it reconvenes in a tennis court, vowing not to disband until France has a constitution

June. **National Assembly** acknowledged as representative of the French people

July. Storming of the Bastille

August. National Assembly publishes the *Declaration of the Rights of Man and Citizen*

August. *Decree Abolishing the Feudalism System*

1791	June. Louis attempts to escape; is captured at Varennes and returned to Paris
	October. **Legislative Assembly** begins session
1792	April. Legislative Assembly declares war on Austria, beginning French Revolutionary Wars
	July. Louis discovered in plot to overthrow the Revolution
	September. **National Convention** convenes, declares establishment of French Republic
1793	January. Louis XVI beheaded
	January. First Coalition declares war against France (Coalition members: England, Prussia, Austria, Spain, Holland, Italy)
	July. Reign of Terror begins; Jacobins capture control of Convention and begin massacring political opponents; tens of thousands killed
	October. Marie Antoinette beheaded
1794	Maximilien Robespierre beheaded; end of the Reign of Terror

1795	**Directory** takes office; becomes a dictatorship by committee
1797	*Fructidor coup de etat* by Directory against Council of Five Hundred
1799	**Consulate** *Coup* of *Brumaire* by Napoleon and two others installs military dictatorship; the Revolution is ended
1804	**Age of Napoleon** Napoleon appoints himself Emperor
1811-1812	Catastrophic invasion of Russia
1813	Napoleon defeated at Leipzig
1814	Napoleon banished to island of Elba in the Mediterranean
1815	February. Napoleon escapes from Elba, returns to France; beginning of 100 Days
	June. Napoleon defeated at Waterloo, Belgium; is exiled to St. Helena in South Atlantic; dies 1821

If you enjoyed this book, please look for the following upcoming titles in *The Best One-Hour History* series.

- Ancient Greece
- Rome
- The Middle Ages
- The Renaissance
- The Protestant Reformation
- European Wars of Religion
- The English Civil Wars
- The Scientific Revolution
- The Enlightenment
- The American Revolution
- The Industrial Revolution
- Europe in the 1800s
- The American Civil War
- European Imperialism
- World War I
- The Interwar Years
- World War II
- The Cold War
- The Vietnam War

To learn more about each title and its expected publication date, visit: *http://onehourhistory.com*

If you could change the world for a dollar, would you?

Well, you CAN.
Now, WILL you?

One Dollar For Life™ helps American students build schools in the developing world, for a dollar. *We can help you build one, too!*

Since 2007, we've built 15 schools and 23 infrastructure projects in countries like Nepal, Haiti, Nicaragua, Kenya, Malawi, and South Africa.

Imagine if you and all of your school's students felt the pride of building a school so another child could go to school. Well, you can! For a dollar.

ODFL will help your club or school organize a fundraiser where *every dollar donated goes into a developing world project*.

Make all of your school's students into heroes! It's easy, it's fun, and it's changing the world.

All profits from
The Best One Hour History™
series go to support ODFL.

Haiti

Nepal

Kenya

You see, you *can* change the world.
Now, WILL you?

Visit: odfl.org
OneDollar ForLife
email: info@odfl.org **Phone:** 661-203-8750

CPSIA information can be obtained at www.ICGtesting.com
Printed in the USA
LVOW08s2029080915

453287LV00033B/1606/P